9.13

Draw Your
P E T !

You Can Draw

Horses!

Katie Dicker

Gareth Stevens
Publishing

Please visit our website, www.garethstevens.com. For a free color catalog of all our high-quality books, call toll free 1-800-542-2595 or fax 1-877-542-2596.

Library of Congress Cataloging-in-Publication Data

Dicker, Katie.
  You can draw horses! / Katie Dicker.
     pages cm. — (Draw your pet!)
  Includes index.
  ISBN 978-1-4339-8744-1 (pbk.)
  ISBN 978-1-4339-8745-8 (6-pack)
  ISBN 978-1-4339-8743-4 (library binding)
  1. Horses in art—Juvenile literature. 2. Drawing—Technique—Juvenile literature. I. Title.
   NC783.8.H65D53 2013
   743.6'96655—dc23

                                2012033136

Published in 2013 by
Gareth Stevens Publishing
111 East 14th Street, Suite 349
New York, NY 10003

Produced for Gareth Stevens by Calcium Creative Ltd
Illustrated by Mike Lacey
Designed by Paul Myerscough
Edited by Sarah Eason and Harriet McGregor

Photo credits: Dreamstime: Rebecca Hermanson 18b, 20, Michael Rucker 10t, Shutterstock: Horse Crazy 18t, Tereza Huclova 26t, Olga I cover, 6b, 8, 22t, 28, Eric Isselée 26b, Lenkadan 4, 12, 16, Julia Remezova 14t, Makarova Viktoria 6t, 14b, Zuzule 10b, 22b, 24.

Printed in the United States of America

CPSIA compliance information: Batch CW13GS: For further information contact Gareth Stevens, New York, New York at 1-800-542-2595.

Contents

You Can Draw Horses!

If you love horses, you'll love to draw them, too! Horses are strong and beautiful. Horses love their owners, and are amazing animals that make great friends.

There are many different types of horses. Some horses, such as Arabians, are fast animals. Others, such as the Haflinger, are used for heavy work while the Appaloosa is great for long-distance riding. Smaller horses, such as Shetlands, are called ponies. They are perfect for younger children. In this book, we'll teach you how to care for different types of horses—and how to draw them, too.

Discover how to draw horses!

⊍ Follow the steps that show you how to draw each type of horse. Then draw from a photograph of your own pet to create a special pet portrait!

⊍ You Will Need:

- Art paper and pencils
- Eraser
- Coloring pens and/or paints and a paintbrush

⊍ Arabians

⊍ Quarter horses

⊍ Haflingers

⊍ Appaloosas

⊍ Paint horses

⊍ Shetlands

Arabians

Beautiful, loyal, and smart, Arabians make wonderful pets. Arabians are muscular and thin, which makes them comfortable to ride. Arabians are also kind, gentle, and respond well to commands. Older Arabians are especially calm and a great horse for children.

Arabians are proud-looking horses.

Step 1

Draw the outline for the horse. Begin with simple shapes. Pay attention to the proportions of the body—this horse has a powerful chest, small head and ears, and a high tail.

Step 2

Now draw the lines where the horse's rear leg and foreleg join its body. Pencil the outline of the chest.

Step 3

Add more detail and shading to the mane and the tail. Also draw the horse's hooves, ears, and eyes, and its nostril and mouth.

Caring for your Arabian

- Horses are very active animals. They love to run around in wide-open environments. Make sure you give your Arabian a large paddock to exercise in.

- Arabians are really smart horses. They get bored very easily and like toys to play with! Ask your vet or local stables about the best toys for your horse.

- Horses are hungry animals and graze on grass for most of the day. Make sure you give your Arabian lots of grass and hay to chew on.

Arabians come in lots of different colors including chestnut brown, black, and gray.

Step

Add some more detailed lines to your drawing. Pencil the muscle lines on the Arabian's chest and back. Draw the lines on the legs and the horse's head.

Step 5

Finally, bring your beautiful horse to life with color. Use a palette of black and grays. Color the face and body a soft gray, then add shade with dark gray. Paint the tail black with gray edges. Color the horse's hooves white with shades of light brown.

Haflingers

The Haflinger is a very pretty horse that comes from Austria. It has a golden coat with a creamy-white mane and tail. This horse is loved because it is so pretty and moves so well. Small and sturdy, Haflingers are calm and hard-working horses.

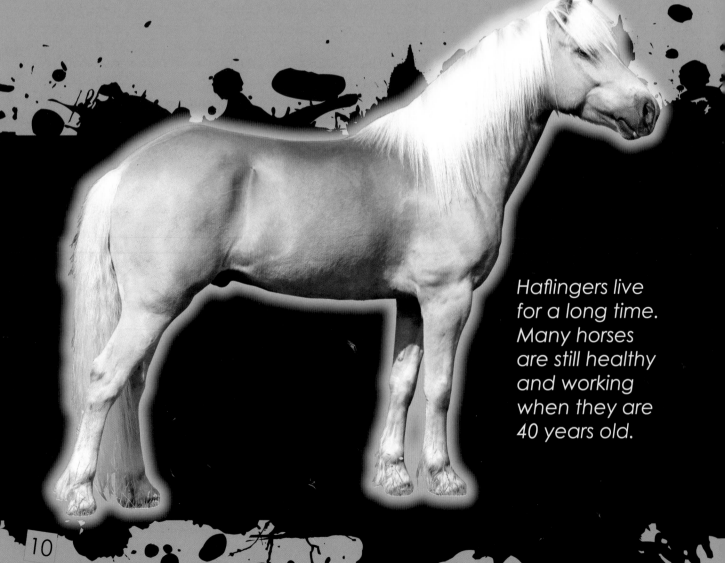

Haflingers live for a long time. Many horses are still healthy and working when they are 40 years old.

Step 1

Draw the outline of your Haflinger. This horse has a long neck and body in proportion to its shorter legs. Keep a steady hand as you draw the outline of the horse's ears, nose, and mouth.

Step 2

Now pencil the tail and the hind legs of the horse. Also pencil in the horse's ears. Carefully draw a tapering, curved line for the horse's rear. Add some light shading to the tail between the legs.

Step 3

Now add more detail. Draw the lines of the horses's mane. Notice how its mane falls forward between its eyes. Draw the horse's nostril, its jaw and mouth, and its eye, too.

11

Caring for your Haflinger

- Haflingers are hard workers. This makes them thirsty! Make sure your horse can always get to fresh, clean water to have a drink.

- Horses are easy to train if you reward them. Give your Haflinger praise if it does something well. Scolding your horse can make it feel angry, so try to keep things positive when you are with your pet.

- Haflingers love company. They enjoy being with other horses and bond with their owners, too. If you can, keep your horse with another for a playmate.

Haflinger foals are just as pretty as their moms!

Step 4

Now add lots of shading to your picture. Shade the body to show the horse's muscles. Add shading to the legs, too. Then draw lots of long, heavy lines on the horse's tail.

Step 5

You can now color your horse. Use a rich chestnut brown for the horse's back and neck. Use a lighter brown for the belly, head, and rear of the horse. Color the end of the nose gray and leave the mane, legs, tail, and part of the face white.

Appaloosas

The Appaloosa is one of the most popular of American horses. It is also one of the oldest. This horse can be seen in ancient cave paintings from thousands of years ago! The Appaloosa is quiet, calm, and very easy to train.

Appaloosas are perfect for trail and long-distance riding.

Step 1

This Appaloosa is leaping into the air. Carefully draw the outline of the horse, and pencil the horse's wild mane and long, sweeping tail, too.

Step 2

Now draw the line of the belly between the back legs. Then pencil the lines where the horse's legs join the body, and add the curving jaw.

Step 3

Carefully shade the Appaloosa's large, black eye. Add detailed lines to the mane and the tail. Draw the hooves and add light shading to the body.

15

Caring for your Appaloosa

U Appaloosas don't fuss about their surroundings! They are happy in a paddock, barn, or stable. One thing these horses love is plenty of space.

U If you keep your pet in a paddock, make sure an adult clears away any poisonous plants or trees from your horse's enclosure. Ragwort and yew especially can make your horse sick.

Some Appaloosas have a patchwork coat, such as this pretty horse.

Step 4

Draw lots of dots for the horse's dappled coat. Add shading to the legs, head, mane, tail, and belly of the leaping Appaloosa.

Step 5

Now color the horse with a palette of grays. Use a dark gray to add some more shading to the neck, belly, knees, upper legs, and the tail. Add some dots of gray for the dappled coat.

Quarter Horses

The quarter horse is one of America's best-loved horses. With its strong legs, it is a super-fast sprinter. This horse gets its name for being the quickest horse to run a quarter of a mile. The quarter horse is quiet and kind.

Quarter horse foals have very long legs and strong, straight backs.

Step 1

Draw your foal in an upright position, with its head facing toward you. Its ears should be pointing upward and its back arched. Pencil the outline of the foal's mane and tail.

Step 2

Now add shading to the horse's mane and tail. Draw the outline of the foal's head, and finish the shape of its ears. Pencil the lines of the legs.

Step 3

Draw the horse's eyes, nostrils, nose, and mouth. Add more detail to its ears, and then carefully draw the hooves.

Caring for your Quarter Horse

- Quarter horses may be fast sprinters but they also love to be lazy! Make sure you give your horse enough exercise, so it doesn't just graze all day.

- Quarter horses love eating and can gain weight very quickly. Keep your horse's diet regular and check your pet's weight with a horse vet.

Quarter horses like to live in wide-open spaces.

Step 4

Now you can draw the lines on the horse's body. Notice the shading around the horse's legs and rear. Add the detail on the foal's knees. Add more shading to the horse's eyes and nostrils.

Step 5

Paint the horse with a rich red-brown color. Use a deeper brown for the areas on the back, rear, chest, and head. Color the mane and the tail dark gray. Leave some areas of the legs and hooves white. Remember to leave a patch of white on the horse's nose and head, too.

Paint Horses

This gorgeous horse is beautiful to look at. With its coat of white and dark colors, it stands out in any group of horses. The paint horse is also stocky and sturdy, which makes it a comfortable ride. These lovely horses are quiet and calm and make great animal friends.

Paint horses get their name because their beautiful coats look like they have been painted on!

Step 1

This paint horse is racing toward you! Be sure to carefully draw the running legs, raised tail, arched back, and upright ears. Draw the ragged mane on the horse's neck, too.

Step 2

Now continue the line of the back to draw the horse's rear. Add the lines of the legs where they join the belly, and then draw the curved line of the horse's jaw.

Step 3

Now shade the horse's eye, pencil the nostrils, and then carefully draw the shape of the hooves. Draw the line of the horse's mouth.

Caring for your Paint Horse

Make sure your horse has shelter from the sun, wind, and rain. A cluster of trees makes a good shady spot, but a stable or three-sided shelter is needed for wintry weather.

Horses stand for most of the day, but like to rest from time to time. A bed of straw or wood shavings will give them a comfortable, dry place to lie down.

Paint horses live happily with other breeds of horse.

Step 4

Now you can draw the pattern on the horse's coat. Notice the large, ragged mark on the belly and the shape on the front of the horse's face and legs. These will be white patches when you add color.

Step 5

Now color your paint horse. Use a palette of rich browns for the body and add dark gray for shading. Color the mane and tail gray and black and paint the hooves gray, too. Leave the patches on the belly, legs, and face white. Your beautiful paint horse is complete!

Shetlands

Shetlands are the perfect riding ponies for young children. Most Shetlands are less than 42 inches (1 m) tall! They come from the Shetland Islands of Scotland so they are used to cold, wet weather. They are strong but gentle creatures, and are easily trained.

Shetlands are very small and cute!

Step

Draw the outline of your Shetland. Notice how long the pony's tail is in proportion to its short body and legs. Carefully draw the deep, round belly and the upright ears. Pencil the tip of the tail.

Step

Continue the line of the belly to where it joins the Shetland's legs. Pencil the lines of the horse's rear legs.

Step

Now add lines for the pony's long, ragged mane. Notice how it hangs over the pony's shoulders and between its ears. Draw the eye and the nostrils.

Caring for your Shetland

⊌ Like other horses, Shetlands need a paddock in which they can graze and exercise. Remember, though—they are small enough to squeeze under a gate or fence! You will need to make sure your paddock is properly enclosed.

⊌ Shetlands are used to wild weather, but it is still best to give them shelter during the winter. They will love a dry area where they can lie down and rest.

⊌ Shetlands have very thick coats to protect them from the winter weather. Use a steel-toothed brush to keep your pet's coat in good condition.

Shetlands look even tinier next to other horses!

Step 4

Add lots of shading to the mane and tail. Add very heavy shading to the eye and nostrils. The nostrils of your Shetland should be large and rounded. Then shade the pony's hooves.

Step 5

Color your Shetland with a palette of creams and browns. Use cream for the mane, tail, and the patches on the face, body, and rear. Use a deep brown for the hooves and to add more shading to your pony.

Glossary

active: moving

bond: to become attached to an animal or a person

breed: type of animal, such as a type of horse

coat: the furry covering on an animal

dappled: spotty

detail: the fine lines and small features of a picture

enclosure: a fully surrounded, fenced in area

environment: area in which something lives

graze: to feed on grass

loyal: to be true to or devoted to someone

mane: the long hair on a horse's neck

nostril: the opening through which something breathes

paddock: a grassy area enclosed by a fence

palette: a range of colors

poisonous: dangerous if swallowed or touched

praise: to say positive things

proportion: the size of one part of the body in relation to another

respond: to react to something

shading: pencil strokes that add depth to a picture

Shetland Islands: islands to the far north of Scotland. These islands can have extremely cold and wild weather.

sprinter: someone or something that can run very fast

sturdy: solid, not easily knocked over

train: to teach an animal how to behave

wood shavings: pieces shaved off wood

For More Information

Books

Clutton-Brock, Juliette. *Horse*. New York, NY: DK Publishing, 2008.

Green, John. *Wonderful World of Horses Coloring Book*. Mineola, NY: Dover Publications, 2005.

Lipsey, Jennifer. *I Love to Draw Horses*. Ashville, NC: Lark Books, 2008.

Ransford, Sandy. *The Kingfisher Illustrated Horse and Pony Encyclopedia*. London, UK: Kingfisher, 2010.

Websites

If you don't have a horse or pony of your own, you can ride your own virtual horse and look after your own virtual stable at:
www.horseland.com

Find out more about horses at:
www.learn-about-horses.com

Discover lots more about different breeds of horses at:
www.ansi.okstate.edu/breeds/horses

Index